MYTH MEN™

GUARDIANS OF THE LEGEND

ANDROMEDA

THE FLYING WARRIOR PRINCESS

BY LAURA GERINGER

ILLUSTRATED BY PETER BOLLINGER

SCHOLASTIC INC.

NEW YORK TORONTO LONDON AUCKLAND SYDNEY

For Laurel, who showed my boys that superheroes can be real. —L. G.   *For my family. —P. B.*

Text copyright © 1996 by Laura Geringer. • Illustrations copyright © 1996 by Peter Bollinger. MYTH MEN is a trademark of Laura Geringer and Peter Bollinger. • All rights reserved. Published by Scholastic Inc. • Book design by David Saylor

12 11 10 9 8 7 6 5 4 3 2 1   6 7 8 9/9 0 1/0
Printed in the U.S.A.   08
First Scholastic printing, November 1996

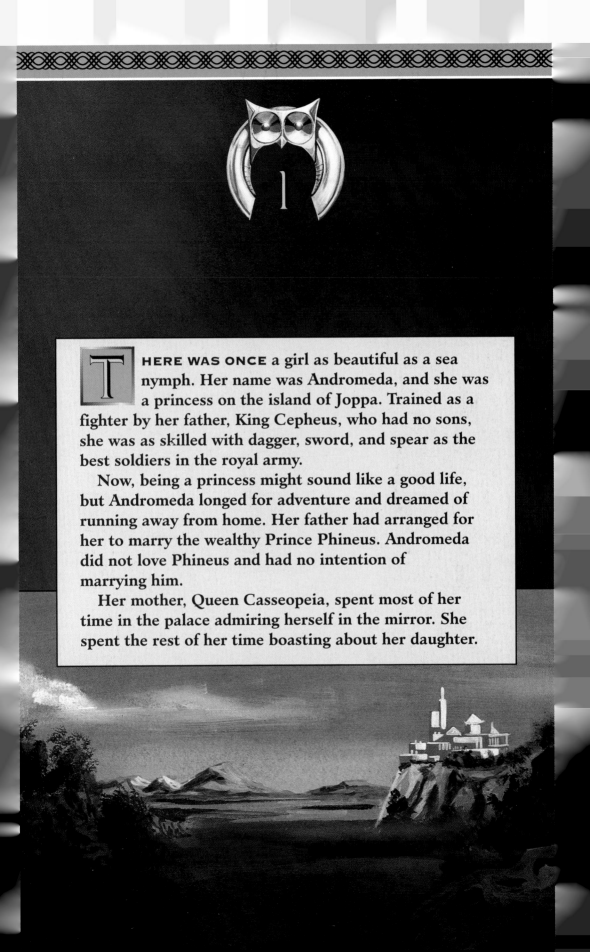

1

THERE WAS ONCE a girl as beautiful as a sea nymph. Her name was Andromeda, and she was a princess on the island of Joppa. Trained as a fighter by her father, King Cepheus, who had no sons, she was as skilled with dagger, sword, and spear as the best soldiers in the royal army.

Now, being a princess might sound like a good life, but Andromeda longed for adventure and dreamed of running away from home. Her father had arranged for her to marry the wealthy Prince Phineus. Andromeda did not love Phineus and had no intention of marrying him.

Her mother, Queen Casseopeia, spent most of her time in the palace admiring herself in the mirror. She spent the rest of her time boasting about her daughter.

But one day Queen Casseopeia went too far. "My daughter Andromeda," she said, "is more beautiful than Poseidon's sea nymphs!"

Now this was too much for the nymphs, who were, after all, very beautiful. They complained to their father, Poseidon, god of the sea, and convinced him to send Cetus, a terrible sea serpent, to teach Queen Casseopeia a lesson.

Cetus tossed ships up into the sky and destroyed palaces with a twist of its spiked tail. Treacherous whirlpools followed its winding path through the ocean and the entire island of Joppa lived in terror of attack day and night.

King Cepheus offered a reward to any man who could defeat the monster. But no man who ventured forth to do battle lived to claim his prize.

2

AS SOON AS the words were spoken, Athena's giant owl swooped down, picked Andromeda up in its claws, and carried her to a great rock, white with surf. Glittering on the top, out of reach of the crashing waves, was a silver helmet.

Andromeda put on the helmet, and, drawing her sword, stood guard, scanning the waves for the black billowing smoke that would announce the arrival of the hideous reptile.

Then Cetus exploded up from the sea, blowing sulphurous fumes and gnashing row upon row of horribly pointy teeth. The gargantuan viper was so long that its coils spread out beyond where Andromeda could see, like an endless chain. Its snake eyes glinted red as blood. And it was coming fast, weaving through the churning water straight toward her!

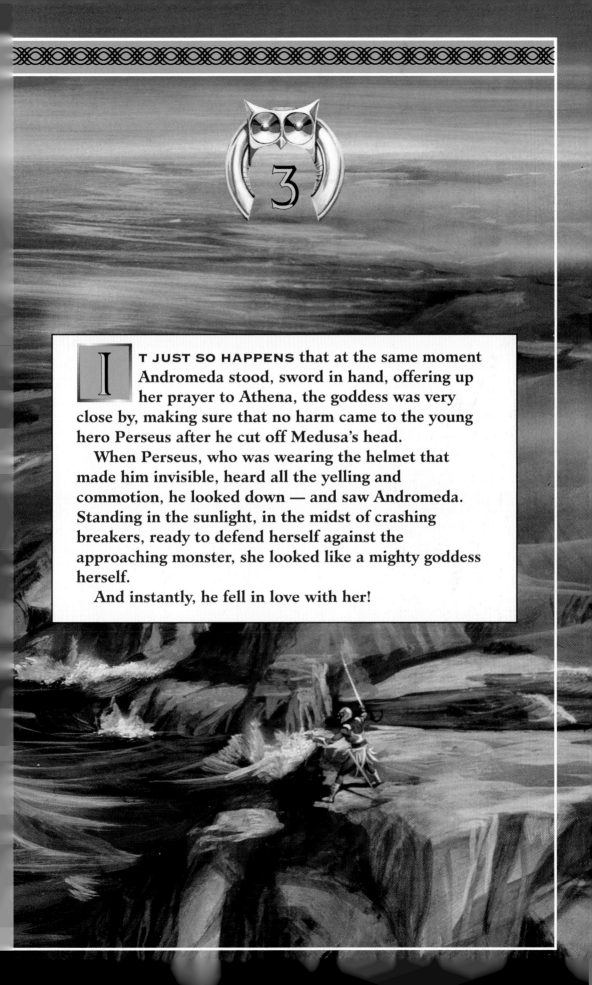

I T JUST SO HAPPENS that at the same moment Andromeda stood, sword in hand, offering up her prayer to Athena, the goddess was very close by, making sure that no harm came to the young hero Perseus after he cut off Medusa's head.

When Perseus, who was wearing the helmet that made him invisible, heard all the yelling and commotion, he looked down — and saw Andromeda. Standing in the sunlight, in the midst of crashing breakers, ready to defend herself against the approaching monster, she looked like a mighty goddess herself.

And instantly, he fell in love with her!

For an answer, Perseus leapt into the thundering waves, pelting Cetus with boulders until it turned away from Andromeda. The serpent bellowed with rage and came speeding toward Perseus, its jaws wide open.

4

THE CROWD, with Prince Phineus in the lead, scattered in all directions, screaming as the serpent came toward them. Belching fumes and fire, it was about to swallow Perseus when the hero flew up into the air, speeding straight to Andromeda. Taking off his winged shoes, he pressed them into her hands.

PUT THESE ON, ANDROMEDA, AND *FLY AWAY.* HERMES GAVE THEM TO ME WHEN I NEEDED THEM, AND NOW I OFFER THEM TO YOU.

THANK YOU, PERSEUS. BUT I *WON'T* FLY AWAY UNTIL THE BATTLE IS DONE. YOU'RE THE *ONLY* MAN I'VE EVER MET *BRAVE* ENOUGH TO STAND BY MY SIDE AND *FIGHT!*

With a vaporous hiss, Cetus veered around, and was bearing down upon them. Quickly, Andromeda put on the shoes and, brandishing her sword, rose into the air. Perseus untied the magic wallet that hung from his belt and handed it to Andromeda.

PRINCESS, I LEND YOU THE MOST *TERRIBLE WEAPON IN THE WORLD* —THE HEAD OF MEDUSA. DO NOT TAKE IT OUT — EXCEPT TO SAVE YOUR LIFE. MOST IMPORTANT, *DO NOT LOOK INTO ITS EYES,* FOR THOUGH YOU'D MAKE A LOVELY STATUE, I PREFER TO FIND YOU *ALIVE* WHEN I RETURN.

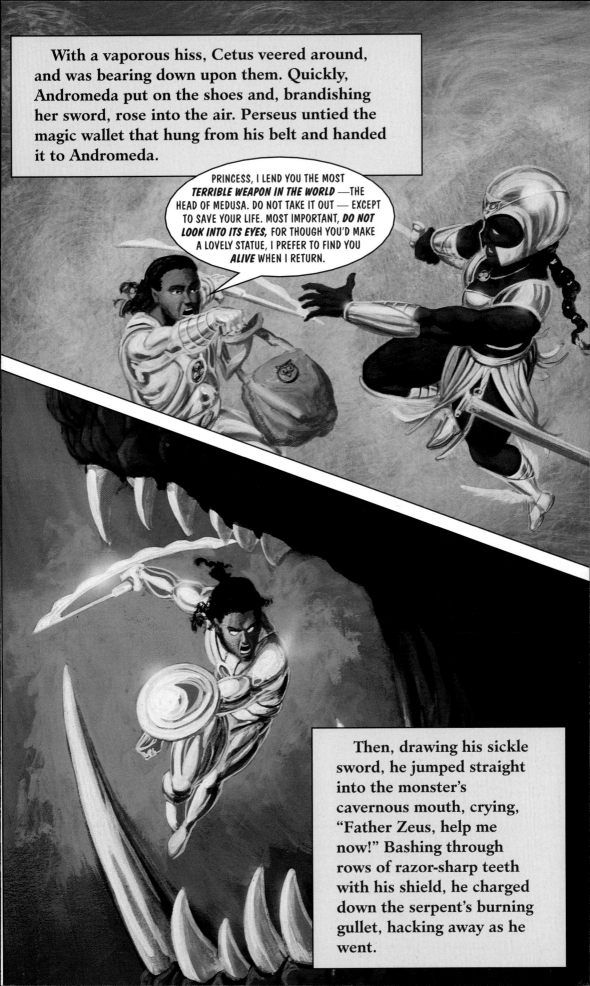

Then, drawing his sickle sword, he jumped straight into the monster's cavernous mouth, crying, "Father Zeus, help me now!" Bashing through rows of razor-sharp teeth with his shield, he charged down the serpent's burning gullet, hacking away as he went.

With a fierce war cry, Andromeda struck with all her strength, plunging her sword into the monster's awful eye. Then she struck again, this time through the neck. Smoke and jets of scorching flame erupted as the hideous creature closed its gaping jaws and, with Perseus trapped inside, dived down, down, down into the deep!

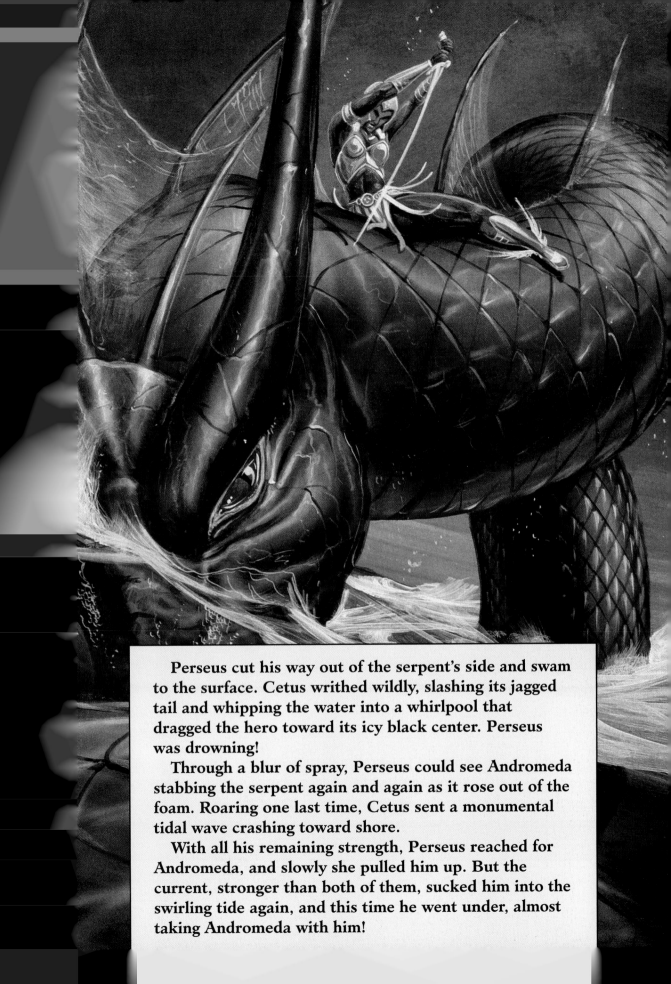

Perseus cut his way out of the serpent's side and swam to the surface. Cetus writhed wildly, slashing its jagged tail and whipping the water into a whirlpool that dragged the hero toward its icy black center. Perseus was drowning!

Through a blur of spray, Perseus could see Andromeda stabbing the serpent again and again as it rose out of the foam. Roaring one last time, Cetus sent a monumental tidal wave crashing toward shore.

With all his remaining strength, Perseus reached for Andromeda, and slowly she pulled him up. But the current, stronger than both of them, sucked him into the swirling tide again, and this time he went under, almost taking Andromeda with him!

But Cetus, too, was sinking! Before the defeated monster could disappear beneath the waves, Perseus grabbed onto it and, using it as a springboard, leaped as far as he could out of the ocean — straight into Andromeda's arms!

Joyfully, the boy with super powers and the flying warrior princess embraced in midair and together flew away.

BUT AN EERIE fog was settling in all around Perseus and Andromeda, so thick they could hardly see one another. The ocean grew unnaturally calm.

"Perseus, are you wearing that helmet of yours again? You've turned invisible!"

"No, Andromeda . . ."

Suddenly, a steely arrow whistled through the air!

Rowing out of the mist, a man in black armor approached, and though Andromeda could not see his face, he looked all too familiar.

PHINEUS! WHERE WERE YOU WHEN CETUS WAS ABOUT TO EAT US ALL?
STAND BACK, ANDROMEDA! MY BATTLE IS NOT WITH YOU.

The hero's moves were so quick, his kicks and punches so swift and hard, that Phineus was down before he even realized he was hit. Then, taking an oar as a staff, Phineus leaped up, knocking Perseus into the water. But Perseus recovered quickly, and seemed so sure of himself, that Phineus became frightened. He had seen the hero dive into the mouth of a sea serpent and live! Perhaps Perseus was no man at all, but some sort of god. After all, he could fly like a god. And he had bewitched Andromeda into flying, too!

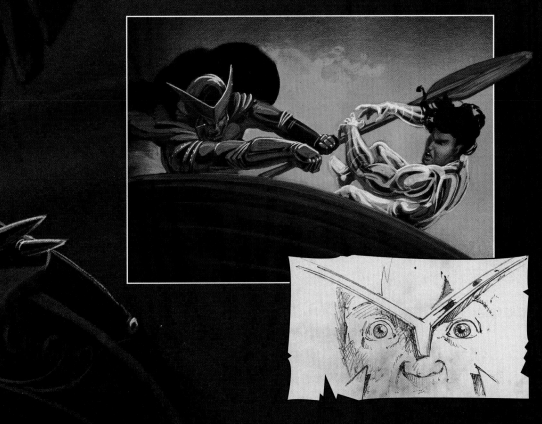

Perseus and Andromeda lay down in the boat abandoned by Phineus and, wrapping their arms around one another, let the moonlit waves rock them gently to sleep. Athena smiled and blessed them, hiding them in a soft veil of mist. She touched Andromeda's cheek and quietly placed in her hand a winged staff. As the light from the staff fell upon Andromeda's sleeping face, the warrior princess was as beautiful as any of Poseidon's divine sea nymphs.

In fact, some would have said she was more beautiful.

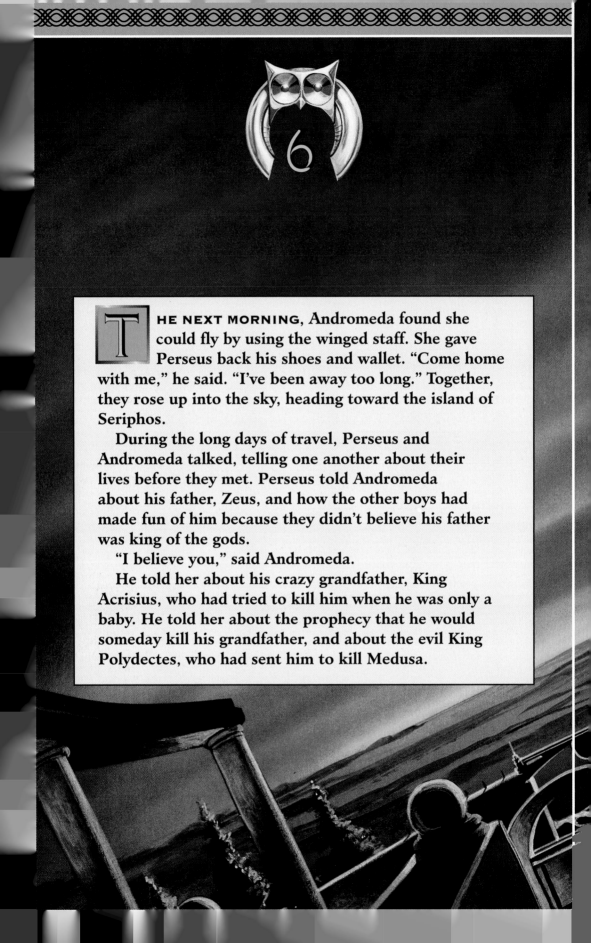

THE NEXT MORNING, Andromeda found she could fly by using the winged staff. She gave Perseus back his shoes and wallet. "Come home with me," he said. "I've been away too long." Together, they rose up into the sky, heading toward the island of Seriphos.

During the long days of travel, Perseus and Andromeda talked, telling one another about their lives before they met. Perseus told Andromeda about his father, Zeus, and how the other boys had made fun of him because they didn't believe his father was king of the gods.

"I believe you," said Andromeda.

He told her about his crazy grandfather, King Acrisius, who had tried to kill him when he was only a baby. He told her about the prophecy that he would someday kill his grandfather, and about the evil King Polydectes, who had sent him to kill Medusa.

As they approached the island of Seriphos, harp music floated out into the night air. Every window in the king's castle was ablaze with light. They landed in a crowd of rowdy young soldiers, standing guard. Among them, Perseus recognized those who had taunted him when he was a boy.

Holding Andromeda by the hand, he pushed his way through to the royal banquet hall where he saw his mother, older but still beautiful, sitting beside an ancient man with a long white beard, who was leaning on his cane and dozing.

His mother rose as if she had seen a ghost and was about to run to her son, but the evil King Polydectes stood in her way.

SO, PERSEUS! YOU'VE DECIDED TO RETURN *AT LAST!* IT'S ABOUT *TIME.* AND WHERE IS THE HEAD OF MEDUSA?

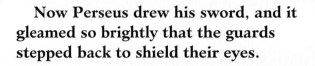

Now Perseus drew his sword, and it gleamed so brightly that the guards stepped back to shield their eyes.

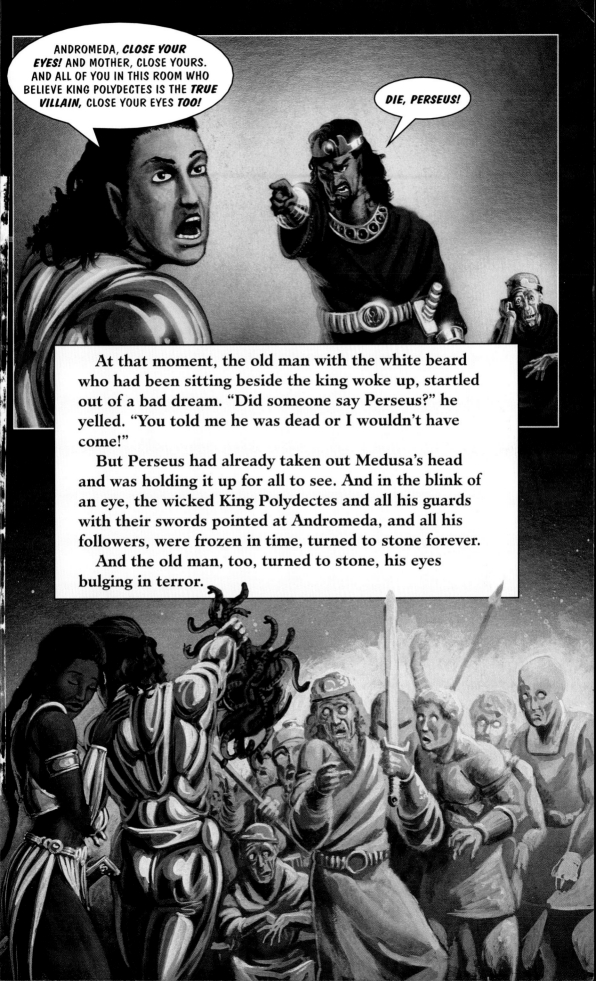

ANDROMEDA, *CLOSE YOUR EYES!* AND MOTHER, CLOSE YOURS. AND ALL OF YOU IN THIS ROOM WHO BELIEVE KING POLYDECTES IS THE *TRUE VILLAIN,* CLOSE YOUR EYES *TOO!*

DIE, PERSEUS!

At that moment, the old man with the white beard who had been sitting beside the king woke up, startled out of a bad dream. "Did someone say Perseus?" he yelled. "You told me he was dead or I wouldn't have come!"

But Perseus had already taken out Medusa's head and was holding it up for all to see. And in the blink of an eye, the wicked King Polydectes and all his guards with their swords pointed at Andromeda, and all his followers, were frozen in time, turned to stone forever.

And the old man, too, turned to stone, his eyes bulging in terror.

7

AS SOON AS Perseus put Medusa's head back in his magic wallet, all those who had hated King Polydectes came forward, hailing Perseus as their king and Andromeda as their queen.

His mother rushed forward, kneeling before the statue of the old man. "The prophecy has come true! Perseus, this is your grandfather, King Acrisius. He was invited here against my will." And although the crazy old king was evil and had tried to kill Perseus long ago, he was still her father, so she wept.

Perseus tried to comfort his mother, but he had one more thing left to do.

"Andromeda, it's time to meet my brother," he said. And hand in hand, they returned to the beach where Perseus first asked the gods to guide him in his quest.

"Hermes, Hermes!" Perseus called.

Thunder rumbled, the clouds parted, and walking on a ray of light, the god sailed down.

"Well done, brother," he said. "Well done."

Perseus handed Hermes the magic wallet with Medusa's head inside. Then he gave the god his shield. And, reluctantly, he returned the helmet as well, but he couldn't bring himself to give back the flying shoes and the sword.

THANK YOU, PERSEUS. THESE GO TO MY SISTER, ATHENA. SHE'S THE ONE WHO TURNED MEDUSA INTO A MONSTER IN THE FIRST PLACE, YOU KNOW.

"Don't go telling *that* old story," said a voice behind them. And there was Athena herself, in armor as bright as the new moon, smiling at Andromeda.

I'LL WEAR MEDUSA'S FACE ON MY SHIELD, TURNING MY *ENEMIES TO STONE.* BUT YOU MAY KEEP THE HELMET, QUEEN ANDROMEDA. I'M *PROUD* OF YOU, MY FLYING WARRIOR!

THE SHOES AND THE SWORD ARE YOURS, PERSEUS! AND, ANDROMEDA, YOU'VE EARNED THE WINGED STAFF. MAY THEY SERVE YOU WELL — YOUR ADVENTURES HAVE *JUST* BEGUN.

And, waving goodbye, the gods disappeared into the starry night.

King Perseus and Queen Andromeda ruled wisely and well. The gods loved them and showered them with blessings. They had many children. And at the end of their long and happy lives, they joined the stars, still together as constellations in the sky.